ludovico einaudi

underwater extra edition

T0039420

all tracks composed by ludovico einaudi
photography by ludovico einaudi

ISBN 978-1-70518-179-9

CHESTER MUSIC

EXCLUSIVELY DISTRIBUTED BY

HAL•LEONARD®

Visit Hal Leonard Online at
www.halleonard.com

World headquarters, contact:
Hal Leonard
7777 West Bluemound Road
Milwaukee, WI 53213
Email: info@halleonard.com

In Europe, contact:
Hal Leonard Europe Limited
1 Red Place
London, W1K 6PL
Email: info@halleonardeurope.com

In Australia, contact:
Hal Leonard Australia Pty. Ltd.
4 Lentara Court
Cheltenham, Victoria, 3192 Australia
Email: info@halleonard.com.au

85mm

LUDOVICO EINAUDI

Con moto, guardingo ♩ = c. 104

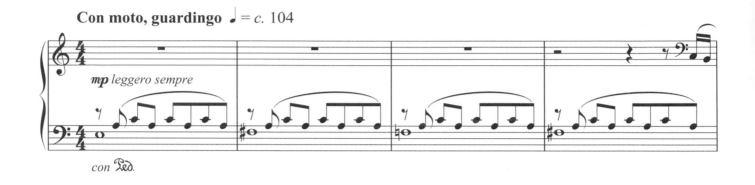

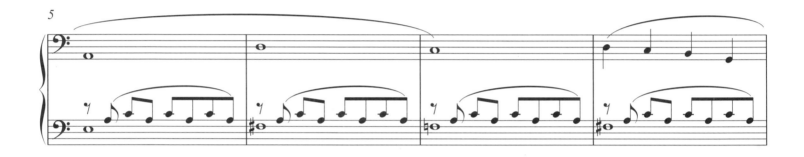

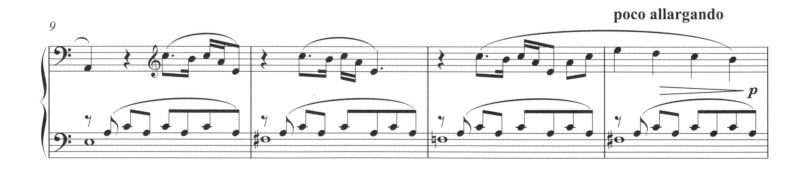

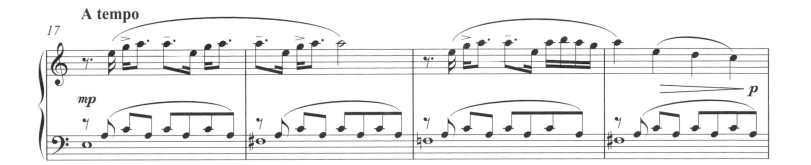

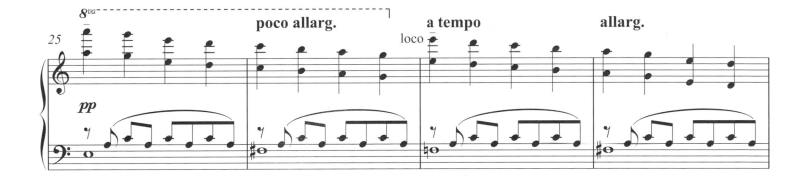

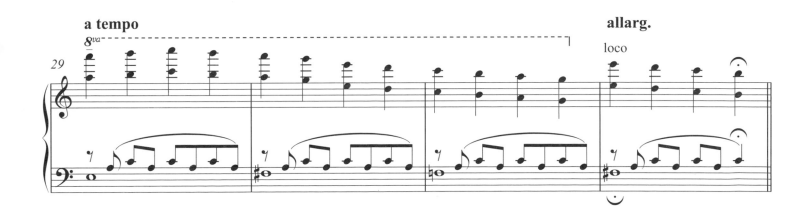

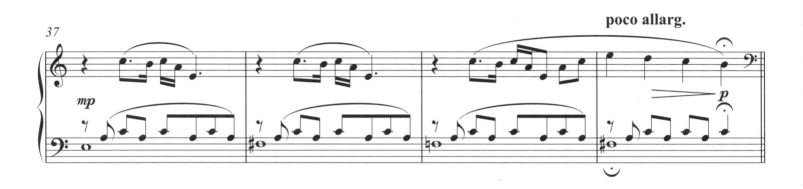

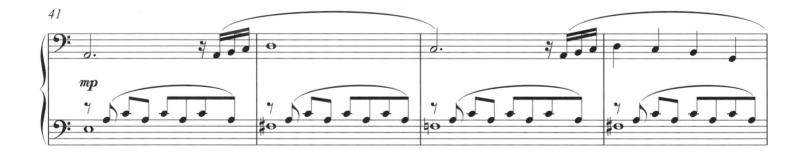

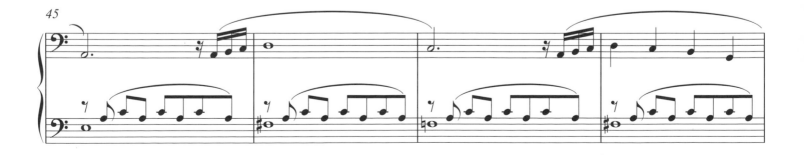

allargando poco a poco al fine

molto allarg.

Adieux

LUDOVICO EINAUDI

Tempo rubato, nostalgico ♩ = *c.* 110

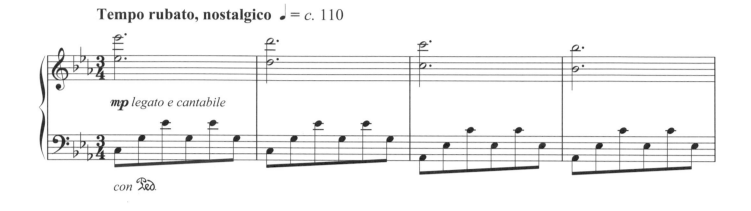

allargando poco

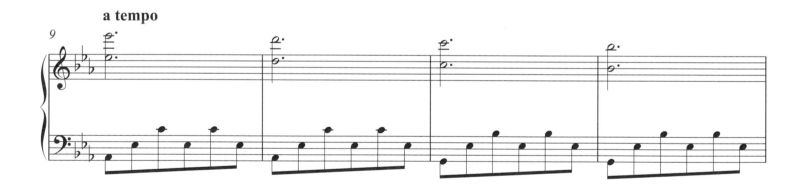

a tempo

allarg. poco

a tempo

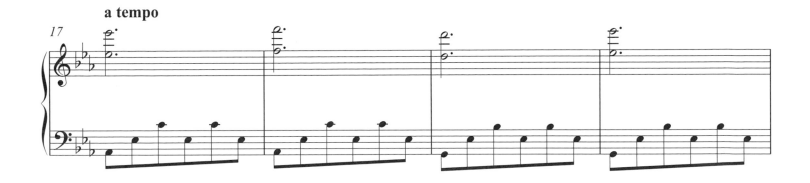

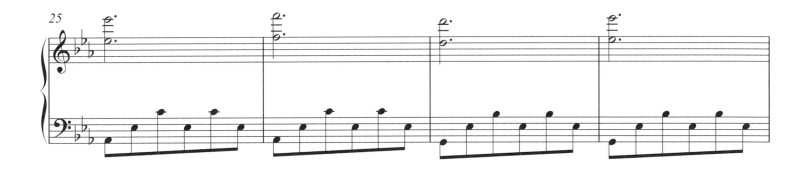

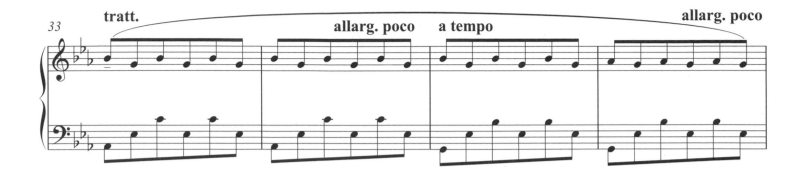

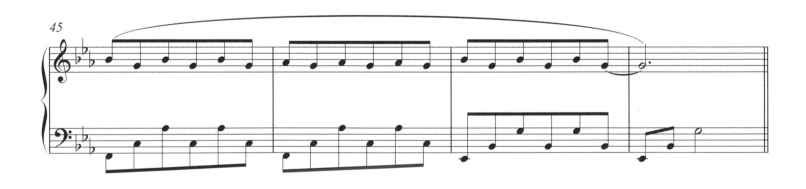

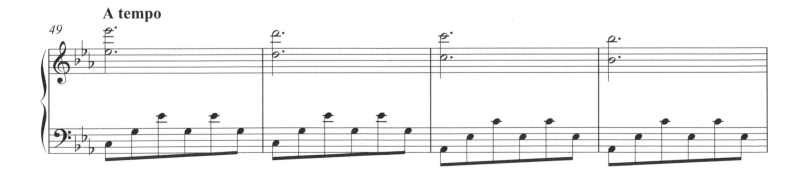

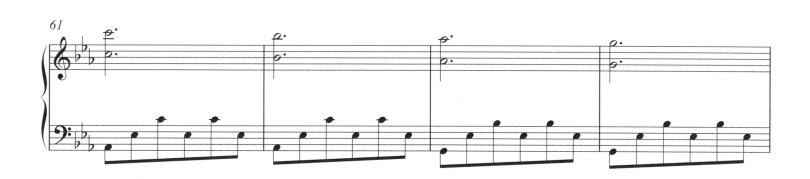

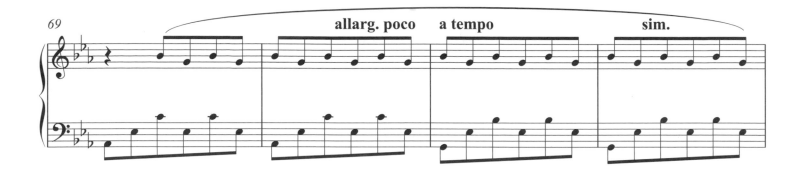

allarg. poco   a tempo   sim.

The Tree

LUDOVICO EINAUDI

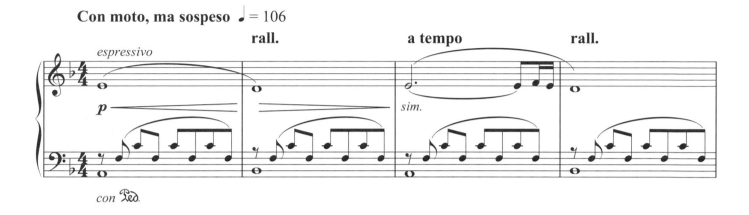

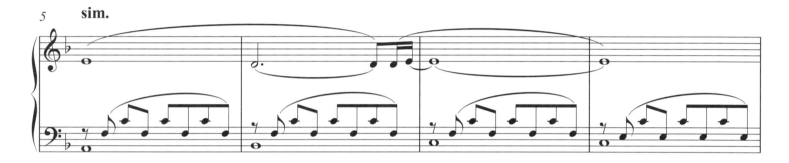

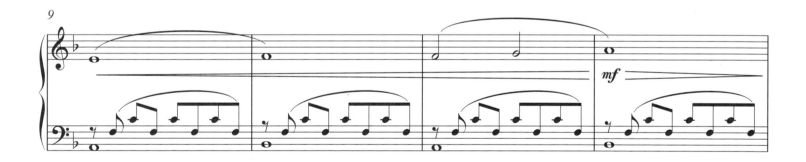

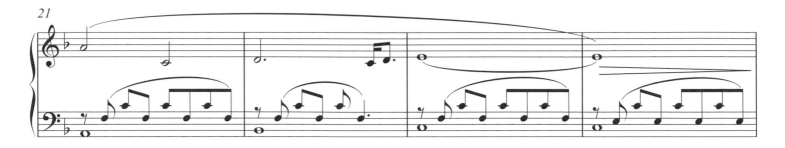

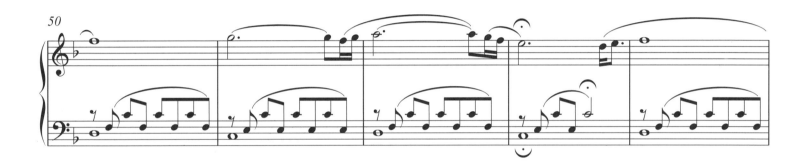

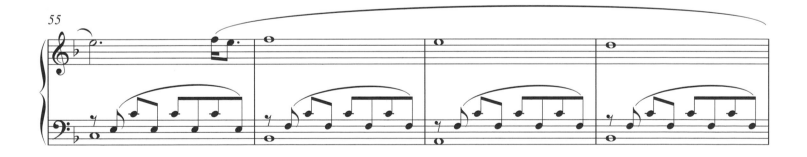

rall. _ _ _ _ molto